WHY NOT US

The Financial Journal for the *Rest* of Us

WHY NOT US

The Financial Journal for the *Rest* of Us

written and created by

Danny Barnes

Published by BlackGold Publishing, LLC in partnership with
The BlackGold Book League of Hampton Roads.

1706 Todds Lane, Suite 258
Hampton, VA 23666

Edited by: Jamel H.
Graphics by: J. Matthews
Designed by: Danny Barnes, J. Matthews

First Edition: August 2024
Printed in the United States of America

This Asset Belongs To

(write your name below)

• Introduction

Purpose of the Journal

Welcome to your Financial Journal tailored for the rest of us! One of the recurring issues I've noticed is the lack of passing down financial knowledge from one generation to the next. It's as if each generation is left to reinvent the wheel when it comes to managing money. I can certainly relate to this struggle. I vividly remember my first encounter with understanding how checks work (don't age me). I was 16 years old and drove over to Norfolk, VA, which was 30 minutes from my house, to visit a friend. At the time, my plan seemed foolproof. I needed gas, but I was confident that I had enough money in my account, so I planned to fill up once I crossed the bridge into Norfolk. However, upon arriving at the gas station, I swiped my card at the pump, entered my pin, and was met with the dreaded message: card declined. I tried again, thinking I might have entered the wrong pin, only to receive the same message. Panic started to set in as I realized I might not have enough gas to make it back home.

I quickly checked my account balance and discovered that it was significantly lower than the day before. It turned out that a check I had written to the local shipyard two weeks' prior had finally cleared, causing my balance to plummet. Feeling bewildered, I called my stepfather to explain the situation, and he calmly informed me that this was how checks worked. In desperation, I asked if he could transfer me the money so I could pay for gas, and thankfully, he agreed. With gas in my tank, I hurried back home.

While issues like mine with checks may not be as common nowadays, many of us still face financial challenges due to a lack of foundational knowledge (such as unexpected subscription fees like Netflix). We were not given the proper financial education in our youth, which can lead to avoidable mistakes later in life. However, this does not mean that we cannot learn and improve our financial literacy as adults. Nevertheless, having a head start can make a significant difference.

I've created this journal to empower and guide you on your unique financial journey, so that you can avoid the same mistakes I've made and navigate towards a smoother financial future.

- Danny B.,

Your Financial Specialist and Guide to a Better Life

Financial Empowerment

What does FINANCIAL EMPOWERMENT mean to you? And yes, that's right, I'm asking *you*. I'm not asking what your friends, your family, or what some financial guru may tell you it is. I want you to completely remove those previous preconceptions of what you thought or heard Financial Empowerment was and *redefine it for yourself*. How I define it is; being able to buy what I want, when I want without having to worry about money, whereas others may see it is as not having to work, while their money makes more money *for* them. Take a few minutes to think about this and write your answer down below. This will be your "W HY" as you move through the rest of the journal.

- **Studies have shown that money does in fact *make you happy*.**
  You don't have to have a lot of money per se - but being able to take care of everything you want to makes for a better and more spirited life.

CHAPTER $1

Setting Financial Goals

1. Setting Financial Goals

"We're talking about practice! We're talking practice... We ain't talking about the game! We're talking about *practice*, man!"

- ***Allen Iverson***

This legendary press conference rant by Hall of Fame NBA Player Allen Iverson brings us to the most important part of building your view of a successful financial future: **PRACTICE**. How many of us are ready to get into the game of building our financial future, but haven't taken the time to properly plan for what that should look like? As they say, those that fail to plan, *plan to fail*. Well, that stops now! In the next few pages, you will decide what matters for you in your financial life, as well as identify and prioritize your short- and long-term goals.

1.1 What do you spend money on?

In the following exercise, you will list the things you currently spend your money on and what you would love to spend your money on. For example, you may *like* watching TV, but you may *love* trying different restaurants. This will give you an idea of what truly matters to you, so that you can best focus your efforts (and money) on what matters. *Begin using the box below*:

What do you currently spend your money on? (Your likes!)	**Now, what *would* you love to spend your money on?**

1.2 Short Term and Long-Term Goals

A part of setting your financial goals is to create short term and long-term goals. **Short term goals** are goals you wish to accomplish within a year. An example would be saving up for a trip for your birthday. On the other hand, **Long term goals** are goals you wish to accomplish a year and on. An example of this would be purchasing a home.

In the exercise below, take some time to list some of your short- and long-term goals. When we have something to aim for, it usually gives us that extra oomph to keep pushing.

Short term Goals (Less than a year)	Long term goals (year and on)

1.3 Prioritizing Goals

Now that you have set your goals from the previous exercise, it is time to place them in the order of importance that matters most to YOU. *Really take your time with this one*, because a rushed order can be the difference between a smooth or bumpy road on your journey to your financial success.

1. ______________________________

2. ______________________________

3. ______________________________

4. ______________________________

5. ______________________________

6. ______________________________

7. ______________________________

8. ______________________________

9. ______________________________

10. ______________________________

Reflection Question

Which goals are a must for me to complete, and how do I plan on accomplishing them?

CHAPTER $2

Income Tracking

2. Income Tracking

"If we command our wealth, we shall be rich and free. If our wealth commands us, we are poor indeed."

—Edmund Burke

My first job at 16 years old was working at Busch Gardens in Williamsburg, VA as a cashier. The pay was $8 an hour, and I thought I had made it because the federal minimum wage was $7.25 at the time. With my "huge" hourly rate, I decided to save for a big purchase. I worked so many hours and did the math for what my paycheck should be at the end. Plan set, hours worked, and now it is payday. As I excitedly logged into my bank to see my account, the excitement quickly turned to dread. This paycheck was much lower than I expected, and this must be some sort of mistake. Later in the month, I received my pay stub, and I couldn't believe all the money they had taken from my check before it even hit my bank account. Federal taxes, state taxes, social security, and a few other things I hadn't heard of at the time.

This story leads us to the next important lesson: Income tracking. You should know what type of income you are receiving and what is being deducted from this income. In the following pages, you are going to be introduced to sources of income. Additionally, you will have the chance to break down your income to get a better understanding of your situation.

2.1 Sources of Income

Earned Income

For this book, **Earned Income** is obtained by actively working for a company. Three common sources of Earned Income are **Wages, Salary, and Commission.** (See below)

WAGES	**SALARY**	**COMMISSION**

WAGES	SALARY	COMMISION
Income earned based on an hourly rate The more hours you work, the more money you can earn **Example**: My job as a Cashier at Busch Gardens	Income earned based on a fixed annual rate Pay not affected by the amount of hours you work **Example**: My current role in the military	Income earned based on the amount your sale Pay depends on the number of products sold **Example**: Real Estate Agent

Investment Income

Investment Income is obtained by buying, holding, or selling assets. Three common sources of investment income are Capital gains, interest payments, and dividends

Capital Gains	Interest Payments	Dividends
Income earned by selling an asset Based on if the asset gained or lost value **Example:** Real Estate	Income earned from lending your money to a financial institution Earnings are fixed and delivered on a regular schedule **Example:** Certificate of Deposit (CD)	Income earned from companies where you own a portion of the company (shares) Earnings vary in amount and delivery schedule **Example:** Stocks

Passive Income

Passive Income is obtained without having to actively work to maintain it. Three common sources are rental property, content creation, and a high-interest savings account

Rental Property	Content Creation	High-Yield Savings Account
Income earned by leasing out property to tenants Earnings depend on occupancy of property and market conditions **Example:** AirBNB	Income earned from intellectual property Earnings depend on how many people you attract to your content **Example:** Blogging	Income earned by saving your money in a savings account that generates more interest than a typical savings account Earnings depend the interest rate and how long you keep your money in the account **Example:** Capital One 360 Performance 360 Savings

2.2 Income Breakdown

In this exercise, you will use the website SmartAsset.com to determine your gross and net income and then input your results in the chart below. This will give you a comprehensive view of your overall earnings. (What are you waiting for? *Head on over to the website*!)

Website: https://smartasset.com/taxes/paycheck-calculator

Categories	Amount
GROSS INCOME (Before deductions)	
TAXES (Federal, State, Local)	
FICA and State Insurance (Social Security, Medicare, Disability,etc)	
Pre-Tax Deductions (Medical, Dental, 401(k),etc)	
Post-Tax Deductions (Retirement, Education plans, Wage garnishment, etc)	
Net Income (take home pay)	

Website: https://smartasset.com/taxes/paycheck-calculator

Categories	Amount
GROSS INCOME (Before deductions)	
TAXES (Federal, State, Local)	
FICA and State Insurance (Social Security, Medicare, Disability,etc)	
Pre-Tax Deductions (Medical, Dental, 401(k),etc)	
Post-Tax Deductions (Retirement, Education plans, Wage garnishment, etc)	
Net Income (take home pay)	

Website: https://smartasset.com/taxes/paycheck-calculator

Categories	Amount
GROSS INCOME (Before deductions)	
TAXES (Federal, State, Local)	
FICA and State Insurance (Social Security, Medicare, Disability,etc)	
Pre-Tax Deductions (Medical, Dental, 401(k),etc)	
Post-Tax Deductions (Retirement, Education plans, Wage garnishment, etc)	
Net Income (take home pay)	

Website: https://smartasset.com/taxes/paycheck-calculator

Categories	Amount
GROSS INCOME (Before deductions)	
TAXES (Federal, State, Local)	
FICA and State Insurance (Social Security, Medicare, Disability,etc)	
Pre-Tax Deductions (Medical, Dental, 401(k),etc)	
Post-Tax Deductions (Retirement, Education plans, Wage garnishment, etc)	
Net Income (take home pay)	

Reflection Question

What are some other ways I could generate extra income? Is there a hobby or passion that I always wanted to pursue? (List them below)

CHAPTER $3

Budgeting

3. Budgeting

"Don't tell me where your priorities are. Show me where you spend your money and I'll tell you what they are."

—James W. Frick

My wife and I used to receive our paychecks, pay our bills, and seemingly spend little of what was left. Yet, at the end of each month, we couldn't figure out where our money had gone and had nothing to show for it. This went on for many months until we finally said enough is enough. We researched on YouTube and eventually settled on YNAB (You Need A Budget) for our budgeting needs. From this one decision, we now know where every dollar goes. In this section, you will learn about the types of budgets and how to create a realistic budget.

3.1Three Types of Budgets

Zero- Based	**Pay-Yourself-First**	**Envelope System**

<u>Zero-Based Budgeting</u>: Every dollar is assigned a specific purpose, so your income minus your expenses equals zero. This helps ensure that every dollar is accounted for and prevents overspending. <u>Pay-Yourself-First Budgeting:</u> Prioritizes saving and investing by allocating money to these areas before covering other expenses. This encourages building savings and investments as a primary goal. <u>Envelope System:</u> Physical cash is divided into envelopes labeled for different spending categories (e.g., groceries, entertainment). This helps control indulgent over spending.

Zero- Based	Pay-Yourself-First	Envelope System
Income-expenses = 0 Best if you have a set income each month. Overspending: Can move money from one category to another to compensate	Set specific amount aside each month for savings and debt repayment; spend remainder how you want Best if you have issues saving each month Overspending: Helps avoid	Divide money into separate envelopes (physical/virtual) Best if you have a set income each month. Overspending: Can move money from one category to another to compensate

Just throw it in the bag!

***Well,* in this case the envelope .**

3.2 Creating a Realistic Budget

A good way to create a realistic budget is to use the **50/30/20 Rule**. The 50/30/20 rule places a certain percentage of your after-tax income into certain categories. The categories are as follows; **Needs, Wants and Savings.**

Needs (50%)	Wants (30%)	Savings (20%)
The essentials that would be hard to live without **Examples**: Rent/Mortgage Utilities Transportation Groceries	Things that you choose to spend money one **Examples**: Fast Food Shopping Holidays Fitness	Savings Goals or debt **Examples**: Emergency Fund House Payment Wedding Credit Card

1) Use the following link to see how the 50/30/20 rule would apply to you: https://www.nerdwallet.com/article/finance/budget-worksheet

2) Download the 50/30/20 Excel spreadsheet (If you would like a manual copy): https://www.nerdwallet.com/assets/blog/wp-content/uploads/2018/12/Budget+Worksheet.xlsx?trk=downloads&

Reflection Question

Based on my likes and loves from Chapter 1, Does my budget reflect that I am spending more towards my loves or my likes? List them all with expenses included below.

CHAPTER $4

Savings Strategy

4 Savings Strategy

"The quickest way to double your money
is to fold it in half and put it in your pocket."

—Will Rogers

When is the last time you saved for anything? For me, that answer would have been *never*. In today's world of credit cards and the "Buy-Now-Pay-Later," saving can be a literal pain. But I challenge you to ponder this precise question; "**If you were able to pay the amount over time, couldn't you have saved up over time as well and avoided any applicable interest**?" I know… I see you thinking about it. But let's not just stuck on that because there's also saving for an emergency fund and other events such as weddings or other goals. As you move into the next few pages, you will learn how to maximize your savings to reach those and other goals.

4.1 Emergency Fund

Let's set the scene. Everything is going well; the sun is shining, and you're driving to work without a worry in the world. Suddenly, you hear a weird sound coming from the right side of your car and pull over. When you check, you find two flat tires with nails in the sidewall. The first thing that comes to mind is, "This is the last thing I needed. How am I going to pay for this?" The answer to your unexpected stress is an emergency fund.

An emergency fund is money set aside for unexpected events or emergencies. Common uses include automobile repairs, medical bills, loss of employment, and so on. You might be wondering, "How much should I put into an emergency fund?" The rule of thumb is to save at least three to six months of expenses, but it depends on your situation. Below, we detail some steps for getting started with building an emergency fund and provide a chart to track your progress.

Emergency Fund Starter Kit:

1) Start with a small goal, for example saving a $1000.
2) Open a high interest savings account at a different bank than your primary bank (ie. Capital One) and link the account to your primary bank.
3) Contribute, small regular contributions to the savings account.
4) Once you reach the initial goal, set another goal for what you feel is attainable.

5)

$1,000 Emergency Fund

HOW IT WORKS:

Each block represents $25. As you save, color them in and keep track of your progress!

WANT A BOOST?

Sell unwanted or unused items to help you reach your goal faster! Color in the items along the path that you've sold or draw your own!

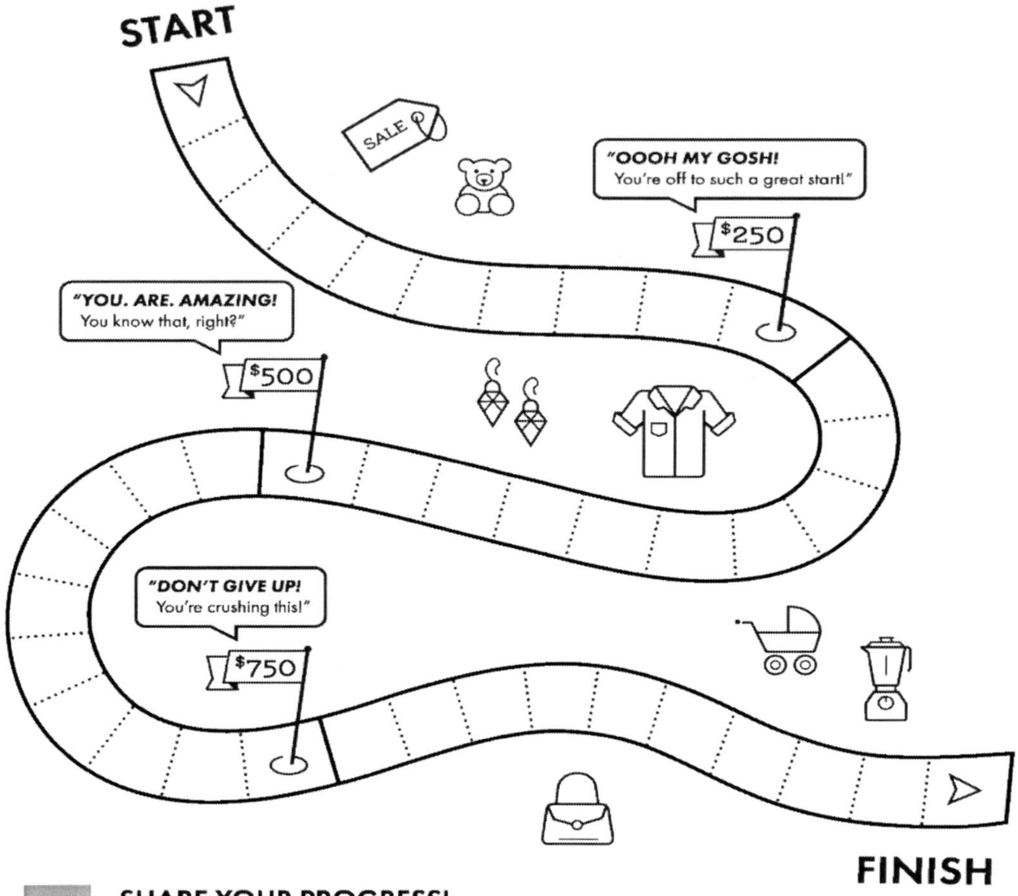

SHARE YOUR PROGRESS!
#sheworkshardsavingmoney

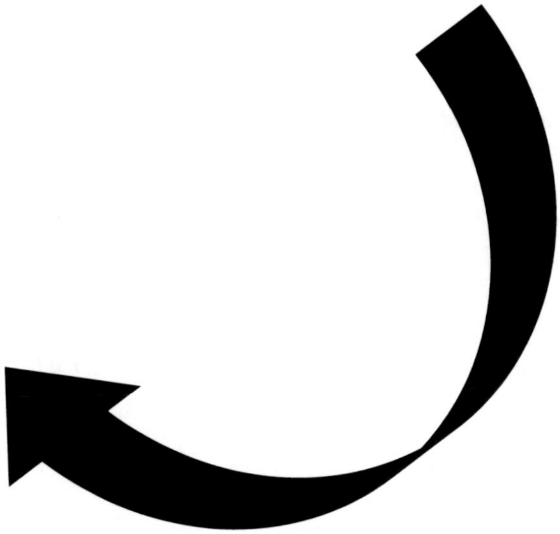

4.2 Saving for Future Goals

Just saving for emergencies wouldn't be any fun, so you should also save for other goals you may have. Examples include weddings, college, vacations, etc. Saving for these goals works the same way as the emergency fund: set a small goal, open a high-interest savings account, make small, regular contributions, and set new goals as needed. Below, you will find another chart to track these goals.

SAVINGS *Goal*

Saving for: ____________________

Amount: ____________________

Target Date: ____________________

Week / Month	Goal	Actual	Remaining	Notes
	Total			

Reflection Question

Besides my emergency fund, what are some other goals I would like to save for? (Vacation, wedding, etc)

CHAPTER $5

Retirement

5. Retirement

“Retirement is the only time in your life when time no longer equals money.”

—Unknown

Hey, listen… I don’t know about you, but I am **tired of working**. Tired of the deadlines, tired of the commute, tired of being in the office, and **so** tired of the many other gripes and complaints of the daily grind. However, all of this work isn’t for naught. Crazy to think about, but we are actually working so that we don’t have to work sometime in the future. This crazy idea of not working is called **Retirement**, and it comes in two oh so sweet flavors**: Employer Sponsored and Individual**. And *Yes*, you can contribute to both types at the same time.

5.1 Retirement Accounts

Employer Sponsored

- Automatically deducts a specified percentage from your wages or salary and places it into a retirement account
- Employer may match your contributions or make a flat contribution

Individual Retirement Account (IRA)

- You control how you save for retirement
- Tend to have more investment options

((Following Pages: 1st Graph is Employer Sponsored, 2nd Graph is IRA))

401(k)	403(b)	457(b)	SIMPLE 401(k)	SIMPLE IRA (No Roth Option)
Traditional: pre-tax contributions, lowers taxable income, withdrawals taxed	Traditional: pre-tax contributions, lowers taxable income, withdrawals taxed	Traditional: pre-tax contributions, lowers taxable income, withdrawals taxed	Employers must provide a contribution	Employers must provide a contribution
Roth: after-tax contributions, no tax savings, withdrawals not taxed	Roth: after-tax contributions, no tax savings, withdrawals not taxed	Roth: after-tax contributions, no tax savings, withdrawals not taxed	Employee owns if they leave the company	Employee owns if they leave the company
For employees of private, for profit companies	For employees of public schools, government, non-profit orgs	For state and local government employees	For employees working at companies with less than 100 workers	For employees working at companies with less than 100 workers
2024 Contribution Limit: $23,000; additional $7,500 in catch-up if 50 and older	2024 Contribution Limit: $23,000 additional $7,500 in catch-up if 50 and older	2024 Contribution Limit: $23,000 additional $7,500 in catch-up if 50 and older	2024 Contribution Limit: $16,000 additional $3,500 in catch-up if 50 and older	2024 Contribution Limit: $16,000 additional $3,500 in catch-up if 50 and older
10% early withdrawal fee before age 59 ½	10% early withdrawal fee before age 59 ½	No early withdrawal fee	10% early withdrawal fee before age 59 ½	10% early withdrawal fee before age 59 ½

IRA	Simplified Employee Pension (SEP) IRA	Solo 401(k)	Spousal IRA
Has traditional and Roth option	Mix between IRA and 401(k)	Can make contributions as both an employee and employee	Allows working spouse to contribute to an IRA for non-working spouse
For the everyday person	For the self-employed, small business owners, some employees of small businesses	For self-employed individuals and solo entrepreneurs	Traditional or Roth option
2024 contribution limit: $7,000; additional $1,000 if 50 and older	2024 Contribution Limit: $69,000 (no more than 25% of compensation)	Employee: 2024 Contribution Limit: $23,000 additional $7,500 in catch-up if 50 and older Employer: Additional 25 percent of your compensation up to limits above	For non-working spouses who have not earned income for the year
Max contribution: Single: modified adjusted gross must be less than $146,000 Married filing jointly: Modified adjusted gross must be between $230,000 and $240,000			2024 contribution limit: $7,000; additional $1,000 if 50 and older Married filing jointly: Modified adjusted gross must be between $230,000 and $240,000
10% early withdrawal fee before age 59 ½	10% early withdrawal fee before age 59 ½	10% early withdrawal fee before age 59 ½	10% early withdrawal fee before age 59 ½

5.2 Retirement Calculator

You can use a retirement calculator to see if you are on the right track in saving for your retirement. Based on your inputted goals – This tool will allow you to see if you are contributing the correct amount or if you may need to contribute a little more.

If you are more an Excel person, I have also added a link to an Excel spreadsheet

Retirement Calculator: https://www.bankrate.com/retirement/retirement-plan-calculator/

Excel: https://moneyfortherestofus.com/am-i-saving-enough-retirement-planning-spreadsheet/

Reflection Question

What does my ideal retirement life look like?
Feel free to draw it out in the box below if it helps you better visualize it.

CHAPTER $6

Investment Portfolio

6. Investment Portfolio

"It does not matter how slowly you go as long as you do not stop."

—Confucius

I was taking a finance class as part of the military transition process, and the instructor mentioned owning stock in Tesla, Amazon, Google, and other major companies. I was so amazed by this that I had to get a piece of the action. I picked some of the same stocks as the instructor but also selected others based on my preferences. Yay! I was officially part of the investing club, but I was wrong. I made two mistakes that day: 1) Investing doesn't just mean picking stocks, and 2) my portfolio was not diversified. To avoid these mistakes, this lesson will teach you about the various asset classes and how to build a diversified portfolio.

6.1 Asset Classes

Stocks/Equities	Bonds/Fixed Income	Cash/Cash Equivalents	Real Estate/Tangible	Futures
Ownership in a company Average annual return of 10% (last 50 years) periodic income known as dividends High risk/ High Reward	Loan made to a company or government Average annual return 5% Provides regular interest payments Low risk/Low reward	Cash, treasury bills, commercial paper Average annual return between 0.01%-3.45% (depends on balance) Interest paid monthly Low risk/low reward	Property, commodities Average annual return 10.6% (residential) 9.5% (commercial) 11.8% REITs Provides monthly income. Risk depends on type of asset	Selling or buying an asset at a future date (ie oil) Return is variable Provides income at a future date High risk/variable reward

6.2 Building a Diverse Portfolio

Diversification is buying different asset classes as a means for lowering your risk. In simple terms, if one asset class is doing bad then one of your other asset classes may be able to make up for the loss. A good way to go about this is to diversify based on your age, meaning being more aggressive in your 20s to 40s and more conservative the closer you get to retirement. However, it is also important to take into consideration the amount of risk you are willing to tolerate.

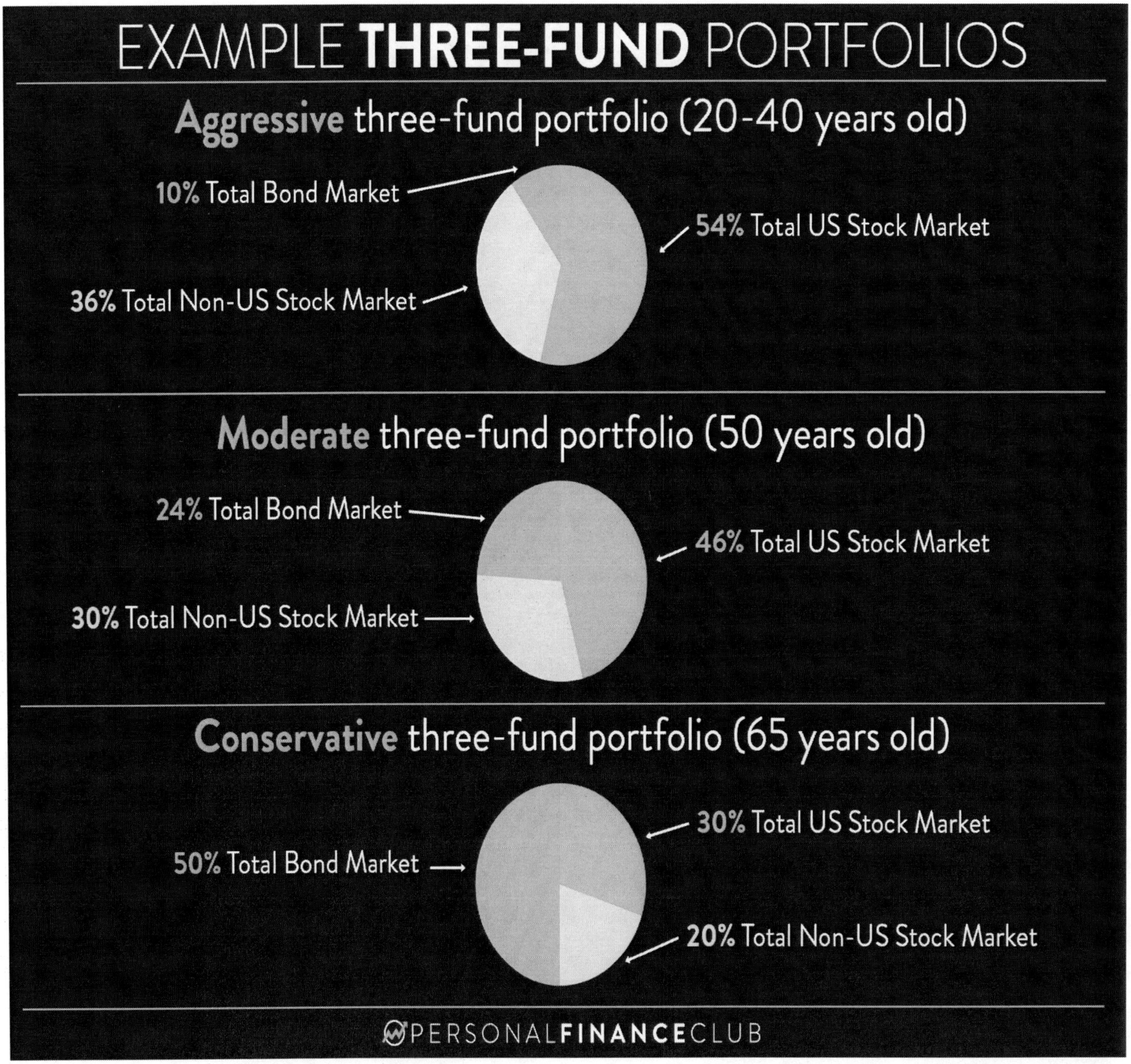

Reflection Question

Investing is not one size fits all. I would like for you to use your Google skills to do more research on your investment options. Use the lines below to write down the pros and cons of each of your chosen options.

CHAPTER $7

Debt Management

7. Debt Management

"Buying on the installment plan makes the months shorter and the years longer."

—Unknown

I remember when I got my first credit card… I told myself I was only going to buy shoes with it and then pay it *right* back off. I stuck to my plan in the beginning, of course, but then I started to see other things that I liked. Before you knew it, I was close to maxing out my very first credit card. I know! This problem not only negatively impacted my credit score, but also led me make even worse debt decisions down the road. In this section you will learn about your **credit score, common types of debt, and debt payoff strategies**.

7.1 Credit Score

Let us set the scene once more. You apply for a credit card on a bank's website, and the first question they ask is, "Can we trust you? *Yes or No*" (though this doesn't happen in real life). You click yes, but then you get a denial because your credit score is 550. Disappointed and curious, you wonder what this credit score thing means…

A credit score is a number that tells financial institutions and businesses your creditworthiness. In simple terms, it lets them know the likelihood that you will pay them back. This score is based on a credit report, which contains information compiled by the three credit bureaus (Equifax, Experian, and TransUnion). A few items on the report are mortgages, credit card balances, auto and personal loans, and so on.

You may now be thinking, "This is all good information, but what is a good credit score, and how do I get there?" **The credit score ranges will be listed below**, and the path to a better score will be explained in the debt management section.

Credit Score Ranges (FICO Score Ranges)

Bad 300-579 --- **Fair** 580-669 --- **Good** 670-799 --- **Excellent** 800-850

7.2 Common Types of Debt

Credit Card	Auto Loan	Personal Loans	Mortgage	Student Loans
Revolving debt No repayment end date Bank/store cards Variable interest rate based on credit score Better for short term purchases	Installment loan Repayment end date For purchasing vehicle Fixed Interest rate based on credit score and length of loan	Installment loan Repayment end date Multiple uses Fixed interest rate based on credit score Better for long term purchases	Installment loan Repayment end date For purchasing a home Fixed or variable interest rate based on credit score and length of loan	Installment loan Repayment end date For education Federal: fixed interest rate Private: fixed or variable interest rates based on credit score

7.3 Common Types of Debt

The section we have all been waiting for and the answer to how you get a better score. Paying off your debt without late payments is how you will improve your credit score. There are two common strategies for accomplishing this task: **Debt Snowball and Debt Avalanche.**

Debt Snowball	Debt Avalanche

Debt Snowball	Debt Avalanche
Prioritizes interest rates Pays off debt with highest interest rate first Move on to next highest interest rate debt after first is paid off Pay less interest over time	Prioritizes balances Pay off smallest debt first Moves on to bigger balances next Builds motivation by paying debts faster

Which one of these are you struggling most with?

No worries, because I've got you covered on the next few pages with the following trackers to help you get out of debt!

Debt Snowball Tracker

DEBT NAME (Smallest balance to Largest)	BALANCE	PAYMENT AMOUNT	MONTHS UNTIL PAID OFF

Debt Avalanche Tracker

DEBT NAME (Smallest balance to Largest)	BALANCE	PAYMENT AMOUNT	MONTHS UNTIL PAID OFF

Reflection Question

What are some strategies I plan on using to avoid rebuilding debt?

____

____

7.4 Financial Education Resources

We all could use a little additional help. So, check out these supplied resources to further educate you and continue to push you to grow both financially and mentally strong.

Books

I will Teach You to Be Rich, Ramit Sethi
Total Money makeover, Dave Ramsey
Money Games, Heidi Ifland Nash
Get Good with Money, Tiffany Aliche
Psychology of Money: Timeless Lessons on Wealth, Greed, and Happiness, Morgan Housel

Websites

Nerdwallet: https://www.nerdwallet.com/
Bankrate (good for calculators): https://www.bankrate.com/
Money and Mimosas: https://www.moneyandmimosas.com/
YNAB (Budget App): https://www.ynab.com/
Quicken Simplifi (Budget App): https://www.quicken.com/products/simplifi/

Podcast

I Will Teach You to Be Rich, Ramit Sethi
Afford anything, Paula Pant
Brown Ambition, Mandi and Tiffany
Nerdwallet Smart Money

CHAPTER $8

Monthly Reflections

8 Monthly Reflections

"Every new month is a chance for growth."

—Danny Barnes

Your financial plan is not a set it and forget it, but an **ever-evolving guide to your successful financial future**. With this mind, it's always good to check in with yourself to ensure that you are still on track in reaching your goals. Below, you will use the five monthly reflection questions at the end of each month to gauge your progress. You can then place your responses in the corresponding month chart. Remember, this is about getting you to where you want to be, not a moment to beat up on yourself.

Monthly Reflection Question(s)

Can I account for where I spent my money this month?

Am I happy with how I spent my money this month?

What have been my biggest wins from this month?

What is the biggest lesson I learned regarding my money this month?

What am I changing that I do with money this upcoming month?

JANUARY

FEBRUARY

MARCH

So it's already March, huh? Guess what – You're done! You did it, you don't have to do anymore.... JK! Keep Going!

APRIL

MAY

Summers coming… How have your financial reflection answers changed so far? Good job. Keep going!

JUNE

JULY

It's getting HOT in hurrr – Or whatever Nelly said. You're heating things up this month. Don't stop! You got this!

AUGUST

SEPTEMBER

We're approaching Holiday Season! How will you prepare your budget this Fall to keep your finances afloat?

OCTOBER

NOVEMBER

The only thing scary about Halloween this year was all those candy costs! And don't get me started on Thanksgiving – Whew! How are you holding up?

DECEMBER

We felt like December needed it's on page and I think you know why! (Saint Nick, we're TIRED!) How did your budget hold up for the year? and how will you be managing your finances as we prepare for a brand new year. Take some time to reflect below.

CHAPTER $9

The "Beginning"

9 The Beginning

Usually, this is where the conclusion would be, but this isn't the end of your financial journey. As I mentioned in the previous chapter, your financial plan is ever-evolving. As you move along in your journey from setting your financial goals to conducting your monthly reflections, be sure to celebrate your achievements. Also, remember that this financial journal is not the be-all and end-all. I wrote this journal to give you a good foundation, with the hope that it will inspire you to go out and do your own research. I have experienced many emotions while writing this journal, but they are incomparable to the joy of seeing you accomplish your financial goals. Here's to the rest of us!

WHY NOT US

Is a financial journal dedicated to the REST OF US that just need a little help in navigating this complex world of ours.

Author Danny Barnes is loving father, husband and a current military member and first-time author from Hampton, Virginia. With a Bachelor's degree in Cybersecurity, he has demonstrated expertise in protecting digital landscapes. Currently pursuing a Master's in Accounting, his diverse skillset reflects a commitment to national security and financial acumen. Follow him on Linkedin:

https://www.linkedin.com/in/danny-barnes

Thanks for reading and here's to financial freedom!

Made in United States
North Haven, CT
05 November 2026

21769184R10033